FORCES OF NATURE

How to Use Your SD-X Reader with This Book

This highly interactive book lets you explore the world in an interactive format. You can read the book and study the maps, photographs, and illustrations, but a touch of the SD-X Reader adds in-depth audio information, word definitions, and learning games to the pictures and maps.

1. Press the Power button to turn the SD-X Reader on or off. The LED will light up when the SD-X Reader is on.

2. Touch the volume buttons found on this page or on the Table of Contents page to adjust the volume.

3. Touch photographs, maps, and illustrations with the SD-X Reader to hear additional information. In a block of text, touch words that are a different color or size to hear a definition or more information.

4. As you touch around the page, you'll encounter games and quizzes. Touch the header or image that started the game to stop playing the game.

5. After two minutes of inactivity, the Reader will beep and go to sleep.

6. If the batteries are low, the Reader will beep twice and the LED will start blinking. Replace the batteries by following the instructions on the next page. The SD-X Reader uses two AAA batteries.

7. To use headphones or earbuds, plug them into the headphone jack on the bottom of the SD-X Reader.

CHANGE THE VOLUME WITH THESE BUTTONS

UP   DOWN

Battery Information
Interactive Pen includes 2 replaceable AAA batteries (UM-4 or LR03).

Battery Installation
1. Open battery door with small flat-head or Phillips screwdriver.
2. Install new batteries according to +/- polarity. If batteries are not installed properly, the device will not function.
3. Replace battery door; secure with small screw.

Battery Safety
Batteries must be replaced by adults only. Properly dispose of used batteries. Do not dispose of batteries in fire; batteries may explode or leak. See battery manufacturer for disposal recommendations. Do not mix alkaline, standard (carbon-zinc), or rechargeable (nickel-cadmium) batteries. Do not mix old and new batteries. Only recommended batteries of the same or equivalent type should be used. Remove weakened or dead batteries. Never short-circuit the supply terminals. Non-rechargeable batteries are not to be recharged. Do not use rechargeable batteries. If batteries are swallowed, in the USA, promptly see a doctor and have the doctor phone 1-202-625-3333 collect. In other countries, have the doctor call your local poison control center. Batteries should be changed when sounds mix, distort, or become otherwise unintelligible as batteries weaken. The electrostatic discharge may interfere with the sound module. If this occurs, please simply restart the product.

In Europe, the dustbin symbol indicates that batteries, rechargeable batteries, button cells, battery packs, and similar materials must not be discarded in household waste. Batteries containing hazardous substances are harmful to the environment and to health. Please help to protect the environment from health risks by telling your children to dispose of batteries properly and by taking batteries to local collection points. Batteries handled in this manner are safely recycled.

Warning: Changes or modifications to this unit not expressly approved by the party responsible for compliance could void the user's authority to operate the equipment.

NOTE: This equipment has been tested and found to comply with the limits for a Class B digital device, pursuant to Part 15 of the FCC Rules. These limits are designed to provide reasonable protection against harmful interference in a residential installation. This equipment generates, uses, and can radiate radio frequency energy and, if not installed and used in accordance with the instructions, may cause harmful interference to radio communications. However, there is no guarantee that interference will not occur in a particular installation. If this equipment does cause harmful interference to radio or television reception, which can be determined by turning the equipment off and on, the user is encouraged to try to correct the interference by one or more of the following measures: Reorient or relocate the receiving antenna. Increase the separation between the equipment and receiver. Connect the equipment into an outlet on a circuit different from that to which the receiver is connected. Consult the dealer or an experienced radio TV technician for help.

Cover art from Getty Images and Shutterstock.com.

Interior art from Encyclopædia Britannica, Inc.; Getty Images; and Shutterstock.com. Select art on pages 7, 13, 30, 32, 34–36, and 56 by Nick LaShure. Select art from Associated Press (21, 27); Jackson County Historical Society (9); Library of Congress (31); Library of Congress George Grantham Bain Collection (19); Library of Congress Prints and Photographs Division (41, 43); NASA/JPL/USGS (53); NASA/JSC (39); NOAA's National Weather Service Collection (15); United States Air Force, Wright-Patterson AFB (9); USDA (30–31); U.S. Geological Survey/T. J. Casadevall (38).

Louis Weber, CEO
Publications International, Ltd.
7373 North Cicero Avenue
Lincolnwood, Illinois 60712

Permission is never granted for commercial purposes.

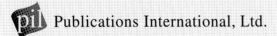

Customer Service
customer_service@pubint.com

ISBN: 978-1-4508-8412-9

Manufactured in China.

8 7 6 5 4 3 2 1

CONTENTS

Introduction 4	Floods 24	Tsunamis 44
Tornadoes 6	Monsoons 26	Landslides 46
In a Tornado's Path 8	Droughts 28	Avalanches 48
Thunderstorms 10	The Dust Bowl 30	Sinkholes 50
Lightning 12	Wildfires 32	Out of This World 52
Blizzards 14	Ring of Fire 34	Predicting the Weather 54
Tropical Storms 16	Volcanoes 36	Disaster Preparedness 56
Hurricanes 18	Epic Eruptions 38	Wild and Weird 58
Cyclones 20	Earthquakes 40	Review What You Know 60
Typhoons 22	Notable Quakes 42	

CHANGE THE VOLUME WITH THESE BUTTONS

UP   DOWN

INTRODUCTION

The forces of nature inspire awe. But they can also bring death and destruction. Every region on Earth has natural disasters—the types and frequency just vary from place to place. Tropical cyclones (also called hurricanes or typhoons) can threaten lives and livelihoods at sea and along coasts. Thunderstorms, tornadoes, hail, and sleet storms may damage or destroy crops, buildings, transportation routes, and vehicles. Storms may even kill or injure people and livestock. Heavy rain can cause flooding, displacing people and interrupting economic activities. The long absence of rainfall, by contrast, can cause droughts and severe dust storms. The violent shaking during an earthquake can cause fires, produce avalanches, and trigger tsunamis. Volcanoes can spew molten rock, gases, and ash into the surrounding area. Extremes of temperature and humidity may lead to the transmission of disease.

❓ WHICH TYPE OF DISASTER?

KINDS OF NATURAL DISASTERS
- METEOROLOGICAL
- CLIMATOLOGICAL
- GEOPHYSICAL
- HYDROLOGICAL

1980 MOUNT SAINT HELENS

1925 TRI-STATE TORNADO

1930s DUST BOWL

2005 HURRICANE KATRINA

1968—73 SAHEL DROUGHT

1960 CHILE EARTHQUAKE

TORNADOES

The tornado has a narrow, funnel-shaped trunk that reaches down from a dark thundercloud and whirls at speeds of up to 300 miles (480 kilometers) per hour.

EARTHQUAKES

The sudden shaking of the ground that occurs when masses of rock change position below Earth's surface is called an earthquake. The shifting masses send out shock waves that may be powerful enough to alter the surface, thrusting up cliffs and opening great cracks in the ground.

TSUNAMIS

Tsunamis are one of the most powerful and feared natural disasters. The large and destructive water waves are triggered by underwater earthquakes or volcanic eruptions.

TROPICAL CYCLONES

The powerful rotating cyclones, variously called tropical cyclones, hurricanes, or typhoons, generate torrential rains and winds of 74 miles (119 kilometers) per hour or more.

VOLCANOES

When a volcano erupts, hot gases and melted rock from deep within Earth reach the surface. The volcanic material may flow slowly out of a vent, or opening, in Earth's surface, or it may explode suddenly into the air.

DROUGHTS

Wherever there is a shortage of rain for an extended period, there is drought. Drought affects plants, animals, and people. It is a serious problem for farmers and for the people who depend on the crops they produce.

1916 TIROL AVALANCHES

2011 JAPAN EARTHQUAKE AND TSUNAMI

1970 BHOLA CYCLONE

2013 TYPHOON HAIYAN

2004 INDIAN OCEAN TSUNAMI

1815 MOUNT TAMBORA

2009 AUSTRALIA BUSHFIRES

TORNADOES

Tornadoes are among nature's most destructive, violent storms. Tornadoes occur when the conditions that cause thunderstorms are unusually violent. Winds blowing in opposite directions around a strong updraft start a narrow, violent whirl. The winds of a tornado are the strongest on Earth. They may reach a speed of about 300 miles (500 kilometers) per hour. Such violent winds can flatten buildings and whip heavy objects, such as cars, into the air.

SUPERCELL

A supercell is a massive rotating thunderstorm that is capable of generating the most destructive of all tornadoes.

HOW LONG DO TORNADOES TYPICALLY LAST?

- 2-3 MINUTES
- 10-13 MINUTES

TRUE OR FALSE?

T | F

WATERSPOUT

A waterspout is a tornado that is in contact with a water surface. Waterspouts typically last for 5 to 10 minutes.

THE ENHANCED FUJITA SCALE

The Enhanced Fujita Scale (EF-Scale) is a system for classifying tornado intensity. It is a modified version of the original Fujita Scale (F-Scale), which was developed by meteorologist T. Theodore Fujita in 1971. The EF-Scale classifies tornadoes based on estimated wind speeds and damage.

EF0
65–85 mph
(105–137 kph)
WEAK

EF1
86–110 mph
(138–177 kph)
WEAK

EF2
111–135 mph
(179–217 kph)
STRONG

EF3
136–165 mph
(219–266 kph)
STRONG

EF4
166–200 mph
(267–322 kph)
VIOLENT

EF5
200+ mph
(322+ kph)
VIOLENT

TORNADO ALLEY

Tornadoes have been reported on all continents except Antarctica. The United States has more tornadoes than any other country (more than 1,000 tornadoes per year have been reported every year since 1990 in the U.S.). Though tornadoes occur in every state, they are strongest and most frequent in the central portion of the United States. This region, known as Tornado Alley, stretches from Texas to Nebraska. Another area frequently struck by tornadoes is found across eastern Iowa, Illinois, and Indiana. While this area sees fewer tornadoes than Tornado Alley does, it has been struck by some of the strongest known tornadoes and has been the site of several large tornado outbreaks. The Gulf Coast, from east Texas to central Florida, has many weak tornadoes. This region is sometimes called Dixie Alley.

TORNADO ALLEY MATCH-UP

Touch a U.S. state on the left. Then touch that state's average number of tornadoes per year on the right.

Kansas	78
Iowa	150
Texas	47
Oklahoma	51
Illinois	48
Nebraska	33
Colorado	57
Arkansas	44

HOW DO TORNADOES TYPICALLY MOVE?

EAST TO WEST

WEST TO EAST

IN A TORNADO'S PATH

JOPLIN TORNADO

Intensity: EF5

On May 22, 2011, a supercell thunderstorm spawned one of the deadliest tornadoes in modern U.S. history. The tornado reached EF5 strength as it moved into Joplin, Missouri, killing 158 people and injuring more than 1,000. The Joplin Tornado cut a path approximately 1 mile (1.6 kilometers) wide and several miles long. With winds in excess of 200 miles (322 kilometers) per hour, the tornado stripped trees of bark, threw heavy trucks several blocks away, and completely flattened many homes. It was estimated that one-third of the buildings in Joplin were damaged or destroyed.

HOW MANY TORNADOES DO LARGE OUTBREAKS HAVE?

- **MORE THAN 20**
- **MORE THAN 30**

WHAT'S THE **RECORD** FOR THE **LONGEST** TORNADO TRANSPORT?

TWISTER TRIVIA

RECORD-BREAKING NUMBERS

2.5 7 1,817 1,300 302 3.5 543

TRI-STATE TORNADO

Intensity: F5

The deadliest tornado in U.S. history traveled through Missouri, Illinois, and Indiana on March 18, 1925. The Great Tri-State Tornado first struck Ellington, Missouri, around 1:00 p.m., catching the town's residents by surprise. The storm quickly moved through Missouri before crossing into southern Illinois. The tornado crossed into Indiana, where it finally dissipated at about 4:30 p.m. By the time it was over, the tornado had destroyed thousands of structures and caused the deaths of 695 people. With winds of roughly 300 miles (480 kilometers) per hour, the Tri-State Tornado lasted 3.5 hours and traveled 219 miles (352 kilometers)—setting records for both duration and distance traveled.

SUPER OUTBREAK OF APRIL 25–28, 2011

Intensity: EF0–EF5

The Super Outbreak of April 25–28, 2011, spawned more than 300 tornadoes, affecting parts of the southern, eastern, and central United States. The majority of the tornadoes occurred on April 27, when a total of 122 tornadoes resulted in the deaths of 316 people across Mississippi, Alabama, Tennessee, Virginia, and Georgia. Of the states affected by the storms, Alabama fared the worst, with more than 230 deaths. One of the hardest-hit areas was Tuscaloosa, Alabama, where a large EF4 tornado passed through the city with wind speeds up to 200 miles (320 kilometers) per hour.

SUPER OUTBREAK OF 1974

Intensity: F0–F5

The Super Outbreak of 1974 was a series of tornadoes that caused severe damage to the Midwestern, southern, and eastern United States and Ontario, Canada, from April 3 to April 4, 1974. One of the largest outbreaks of tornadoes ever recorded, it consisted of 148 tornadoes and resulted in more than $1 billion in damage and 330 deaths.

THUNDERSTORMS

Thunderstorms are a common weather disturbance. These storms are usually violent and short-lived. Thunderstorms can cause a variety of types of damage to people and property. All thunderstorms produce lightning, which may cause fires and fatalities. Other thunderstorm-related hazards include strong winds that can top 120 miles (193 kilometers) per hour, hail that can be bigger than a golf ball, flash flooding that can sweep away cars and people, and tornadoes that can destroy entire towns.

WHAT MAKES A THUNDERSTORM *SEVERE?*

Thunderstorms are classified as "severe" when they produce:

- Hail at least 1 inch (2.5 centimeters) in diameter
- Wind gusts of at least 58 miles (93 kilometers) per hour
- A tornado

WHAT'S A THUNDERSTORM DAY?

TRUE OR FALSE?

T F

WHERE THUNDERSTORMS OCCUR

Thunderstorms are known to occur in almost every region of the world, though they are rare in polar regions and not common at latitudes higher than 50° N and 50° S. Thunderstorms occur most often in the tropical latitudes over land, where the air is most likely to heat quickly and form strong updrafts. In the United States, the areas with the most thunderstorm activity are the Florida peninsula (more than 90 thunderstorm days per year), the Gulf Coast (70–80 days per year), and the mountains of New Mexico (50–60 days per year).

PACIFIC OCEAN

ASIA

AUSTRALIA

INDIAN OCEAN

EUROPE

AFRICA

Equator

ATLANTIC OCEAN

NORTH AMERICA

SOUTH AMERICA

ATLANTIC OCEAN

ANTARCTICA

PACIFIC OCEAN

Thunderstorm Occurrence

5   20   60   100   180

Days per Year

BY THE NUMBERS

Touch a number on the left. Then touch the matching description on the right.

100 — average number of annual thunderstorms in the U.S.

2,000 — average annual number of thunderstorm days in Tampa, Florida

140 — estimated number of annual thunderstorms worldwide

100,000 — average number of annual flash flood fatalities in the U.S.

16,000,000 — miles per hour needed for a severe thunderstorm classification

58 — number of thunderstorms occurring at any given moment

WHAT CAUSES THUNDER?

Touch to find out!

LIGHTNING

Lightning is the visible discharge of electricity released from the atmosphere during thunderstorms. Water droplets and ice particles inside a cloud carry electrical charges. Some of the charges are positive and others are negative. When the electrical charges in a thunderstorm build up enough, the energy is released with a flash of lightning.

MYTH OR TRUTH?

MYTH   TRUTH

LIGHTNING STRIKES EARTH 8 MILLION TIMES PER DAY!

TYPES OF LIGHTNING

During a thunderstorm, lightning flashes can occur within a cloud (intra-cloud), between clouds (cloud-to-cloud), between a cloud and the air (cloud-to-air), or between a cloud and the ground (cloud-to-ground). About one-third of lightning flashes travel from the cloud to the ground; most of these originate in negatively charged regions of the cloud.

⚡ WHICH TYPE?

CLOUD-TO-GROUND LIGHTNING

Cloud-to-ground lightning forms when negative electrical charges build up in a cloud and positive charges build up on the ground beneath the cloud.

CLOUD-TO-CLOUD LIGHTNING

Cloud-to-cloud lightning occurs between the positive and negative charges in two separate clouds.

INTRA-CLOUD LIGHTNING

Intra-cloud lightning is the most common form of lightning. Intra-cloud lightning travels between oppositely charged regions within a single storm cloud. It is sometimes called sheet lightning because a "sheet" of light illuminates the sky.

CLOUD-TO-AIR LIGHTNING

Cloud-to-air lightning occurs when the positively charged air at the top of the cloud travels to the surrounding negatively charged air.

BLIZZARDS

Blizzards are powerful storms that involve strong winds and large quantities of falling or blowing snow. In the United States, the National Weather Service defines a blizzard as a storm with winds of at least 35 miles (56 kilometers) per hour and enough falling or blowing snow to limit visibility to 0.25 mile (0.4 kilometer) or less for at least three hours. Such low visibilities make driving dangerous. A severe blizzard has winds greater than 45 miles (72 kilometers) per hour, visibility near zero, and temperatures of 10° F (–12° C) or lower. The strong winds can create hazardously low windchill values (which make the air "feel" colder than it really is). Frostbite occurs more quickly under such conditions.

TRUE OR FALSE?

T F

DID YOU KNOW?

Not all blizzards have falling snow. Ground blizzards occur when no snow is falling.

THE GREAT BLIZZARD OF 1888

In March 1888, a severe blizzard pummeled the Atlantic coast of the United States. The storm blanketed some areas with as much as 50 inches (127 centimeters) of snow. High winds demolished power and telegraph lines and resulted in snowdrifts up to 50 feet (15 meters) high. Many workers were stranded in the streets, on trains, in elevated transit cars, and at their places of employment. The Great Blizzard killed more than 400 people, including about 100 who were lost at sea.

STORM OF THE CENTURY

Touch a location on the left. Then touch that location's total snowfall during the storm on the right.

ASHEVILLE, North Carolina	**36** inches (91 centimeters)
BIRMINGHAM, Alabama	**44** inches (112 centimeters)
LATROBE, Pennsylvania	**17** inches (43 centimeters)
MOUNTAIN CITY, Georgia	**56** inches (142 centimeters)
MOUNT LE CONTE, Tennessee	**19** inches (48 centimeters)
MOUNT MITCHELL, North Carolina	**29** inches (74 centimeters)
PAGE COUNTY, Virginia	**24** inches (61 centimeters)
SNOWSHOE, West Virginia	**50** inches (127 centimeters)

In March 1993, the Storm of the Century struck the East Coast of the United States with strong winds, heavy snow, and frigid temperatures. Wind gusts were recorded at more than 140 miles (225 kilometers) per hour at Mount Washington in New Hampshire. Record snowfall hit parts of Georgia, North Carolina, and Virginia. Total amounts ranged from about 6 inches (15 centimeters) in Florida's panhandle to more than 55 inches (140 centimeters) in Tennessee's Great Smoky Mountains.

In Antarctica, blizzards are associated with winds spilling over the edge of the ice plateau at an average speed of 100 miles (160 kilometers) per hour.

TROPICAL STORMS

A tropical storm begins as a tropical disturbance. When the wind speed increases to 23 miles (36 kilometers) per hour, the storm is called a tropical depression. Once the wind speed exceeds 39 miles (63 kilometers) per hour, the system is called a tropical storm. If the maximum wind speed exceeds 74 miles (119 kilometers) per hour, the storm is classified as a tropical cyclone.

Tropical cyclones are circular storms that form over warm, tropical oceans. These storms bring heavy rains, strong winds, and a devastating phenomenon known as storm surge. This combination of high winds and water makes tropical cyclones a serious hazard for coastal areas in tropical and subtropical regions of the world.

Tropical cyclones have different names in different places. These storms are called hurricanes when they form near North America and the Caribbean. They are called typhoons in the western North Pacific around the Philippines, Japan, and China. Those near Australia and in the Indian Ocean are often called cyclones. All of these names refer to the same type of rotating storm.

WHAT'S A STORM SURGE?

TRUE OR FALSE?

T F

SAFFIR-SIMPSON SCALE

CATEGORY	WIND SPEED	STORM SURGE
1	74–95 mph (119–153 kph)	4–5 ft. (1.2–1.5 m)
2	96–110 mph (154–177 kph)	6–8 ft. (1.8–2.4 m)
3	111–129 mph (178–208 kph)	9–12 ft. (2.7–3.7 m)
4	130–156 mph (209–251 kph)	13–18 ft. (3.9–5.5 m)
5	Greater than 157 mph (252 kph)	Greater than 18 ft. (5.5 m)

ANATOMY OF A CYCLONE

What parts make up a tropical cyclone?

EYE

EYEWALL

RAINBANDS

DID YOU KNOW?

Tropical cyclones spin counterclockwise in the Northern Hemisphere and clockwise in the Southern Hemisphere.

HURRICANES

HISTORIC HURRICANES

HURRICANE NAMES

The U.S. National Weather Service has a list of names to be used for tropical storms and hurricanes. The list of Atlantic storm names is typically repeated every seventh year. If a hurricane causes extreme damage, its name is retired and never used again.

HURRICANE ANDREW

Category: 5
August 1992

Hurricane Andrew ravaged the Bahamas, southern Florida, and south-central Louisiana in late August 1992. Hurricane Andrew began as a tropical depression off the west coast of Africa on August 16. It became a tropical storm on August 17 and a hurricane on August 22. Andrew made landfall in the Bahamas on August 23 as a category 5 hurricane with winds of 161 miles (259 kilometers) per hour. After weakening slightly over the Bahamas, the storm strengthened again over the Straits of Florida. When Hurricane Andrew struck the coast of Florida on August 24, the storm's wind speed was 166.8 miles (268 kilometers) per hour, with at least one gust reaching 177 miles (285 kilometers) per hour.

GREAT GALVESTON HURRICANE

Category: 4
September 1900

The Great Galveston Hurricane of 1900 was one of the deadliest natural disasters in U.S. history. The system landed on Cuba as a tropical storm on September 3. In the Gulf of Mexico, the storm rapidly intensified. Citizens along the Gulf Coast were warned that the hurricane was approaching, but many ignored the warnings. The storm reached the island city of Galveston, Texas, on September 8, with winds of more than 130 miles (210 kilometers) per hour. Homes and businesses were easily demolished by the water and wind, and thousands of lives were lost.

HURRICANE CAMILLE

Category: 5
August 1969

Hurricane Camille, one of the strongest hurricanes of the 20th century, hit Mississippi on the night of August 17. Camille's gusts were powerful enough to knock out all wind-recording instruments, leaving some experts estimating wind speed at more than 200 miles (320 kilometers) per hour. The storm moved inland across much of the southeastern United States and Appalachia, causing severe flash flooding. Camille dumped 12–20 inches (30–50 centimeters) of rain in parts of West Virginia and Virginia, which experienced devastating floods and landslides.

SUPERSTORM SANDY

Category: 3
October 2012

A massive and highly destructive storm developed in the warm waters of the tropical North Atlantic Ocean in October 2012. The storm swept through the Caribbean area as a tropical cyclone, or hurricane, and became known as Hurricane Sandy. On October 29, Sandy made landfall near Atlantic City, New Jersey, with maximum sustained winds of 80 miles (129 kilometers) per hour. The following day, Sandy merged with a cold air mass, transforming the hurricane into a sprawling **extratropical cyclone**, which was renamed Post-Tropical Cyclone Sandy. Meteorologists and newscasters called it Superstorm Sandy. At its greatest size, Sandy covered more than 900 miles (1,450 kilometers).

HURRICANE KATRINA

Category: 3
August 2005

Hurricane Katrina began as a tropical depression on August 23, 2005. By August 27, Katrina had strengthened into a category 3 hurricane and covered nearly the entire Gulf of Mexico. By the following afternoon, Katrina had become one of the most powerful Atlantic storms on record, with winds in excess of 170 miles (275 kilometers) per hour. After reaching category 5 strength over the Gulf of Mexico, Katrina weakened before making landfall in Louisiana and Mississippi on August 29 as a category 3 hurricane.

Know Your Numbers

28   31   26.5   1,620

7,165   2,500   6   21

CYCLONES

CYCLONE NARGIS

Tropical Cyclone Nargis formed in the Bay of Bengal and made landfall in Myanmar (Burma) in early May 2008 as a category 4 storm. The cyclone struck the densely populated rice-growing region of the Irrawaddy River delta, cutting a wide path of destruction. A 12-foot (4-meter) storm surge obliterated coastal villages. Nargis claimed the lives of more than 100,000 people.

BHOLA CYCLONE

In 1970, the Bhola Cyclone struck East Pakistan (now Bangladesh), killing hundreds of thousands of people in the densely populated Ganges-Brahmaputra delta. Even though the cyclone was not ranked in the top category of cyclone intensity, it was perhaps the deadliest tropical cyclone in recorded history and one of the greatest natural disasters. The Bhola Cyclone, also called the Ganges-Brahmaputra delta cyclone, formed over the Bay of Bengal on November 8, 1970. After reaching its peak wind speed of 115 miles (185 kilometers) per hour, it made landfall on the coast of East Pakistan on November 12. The cyclone was accompanied by a storm surge that flooded the low-lying region. At least 300,000 residents were killed and entire villages were wiped out.

BY THE NUMBERS

4   174

300,000

80   115

71.8   42

TROPICAL CYCLONE INTENSITY

Tropical cyclones are ranked on one of several tropical cyclone scales according to their sustained winds and where they are located. In Australia, tropical cyclones are assigned a category ranging from 1 for the weakest to 5 for the strongest based on mean wind speed and wind gust speed.

CATEGORY	MAXIMUM MEAN WIND	TYPICAL STRONGEST GUST
Category 1 (tropical cyclone)	**39–54 mph** (63–88 kph)	**56–77 mph** (90–125 kph)
Category 2 (tropical cyclone)	**55–72 mph** (89–117 kph)	**78–102 mph** (125–164 kph)
Category 3 (severe tropical cyclone)	**73–98 mph** (118–159 kph)	**103–139 mph** (165–224 kph)
Category 4 (severe tropical cyclone)	**99–123 mph** (160–199 kph)	**140–173 mph** (225–279 kph)
Category 5 (severe tropical cyclone)	**Over 124 mph** (200 kph)	**Over 174 mph** (280 kph)

TYPHOONS

Tropical cyclones—intense circular storms that originate over tropical oceans—are called typhoons when they occur in the western North Pacific Ocean around the Philippines, Japan, and China. Like their sister storms, these tropical cyclones must have maximum sustained wind speeds of 74 miles (119 kilometers) per hour or greater to be classified as typhoons. If a typhoon has maximum sustained winds of 150 miles (241 kilometers) per hour or greater, it becomes a super typhoon.

TRUE OR FALSE?

T F

SUPER TYPHOON HAIYAN

Super Typhoon Haiyan, known locally as Yolanda, made landfall in the central Philippines on November 8, 2013, with maximum sustained winds of 195 miles (314 kilometers) per hour—the highest wind speed ever recorded at landfall. The tropical cyclone produced high winds, coastal storm surges, heavy rains, and flooding in the land areas over which it passed. The Philippines is made up of more than 7,000 islands along the western rim of the Pacific Ocean in an area known for spawning many tropical storms. Because of its location and abundance of exposed coast, the Philippines is especially prone to typhoons. After crossing through the central Philippines, Haiyan emerged over the South China Sea and gradually weakened before striking Vietnam and China.

NUMBER MATCHING

Touch a number on the left. Then touch the matching description on the right.

195	number of people displaced by Typhoon Haiyan
39	average number of typhoons per year in Northwest Pacific basin
4,000,000	miles per hour needed for a super typhoon classification
16.5	average number of annual tropical storms in Northwest Pacific basin
150	miles per hour of Haiyan's maximum sustained winds
26	number of days the longest-lasting tropical cyclone lasted
1,000,000	number of homes damaged or destroyed by Haiyan
31	number of named storms in Northwest Pacific basin in 1964

TYPHOON NAMES

Pacific and Indian basin storms are named according to systems established by regional committees. In the western North Pacific and South China Sea, the names on the official list come from the different countries or regions within the committee. Names submitted by each country range from personal names to descriptive terms to names of animals and plants.

WHICH COUNTRY CONTRIBUTED THE NAME HAIYAN?

FLOODS

Floods can occur during excessive rains, when snow or ice melts too quickly, when ocean water comes on land, or when dams or levees break. Most floods take hours or days to develop. But flash floods can develop in a matter of minutes and with little warning, making them particularly deadly.

Major floods can be catastrophic, killing and injuring great numbers of people and destroying homes, businesses, hospitals, and schools. In 1931, more than 3.5 million people died as a result of flooding and subsequent starvation and disease after heavy rains caused China's Yangtze River to overflow its banks.

Not all floods are bad. A river's floodwaters can deposit minerals and organic materials onto the surrounding land, making it more fertile for farming. People in ancient Egypt depended on the flooding of the Nile River every year to help them grow their crops.

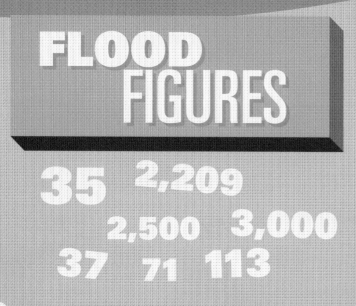

Thames Barrier

FLOOD FIGURES

35   2,209
    2,500   3,000
37   71   113

FLOOD CONTROL

In ancient times, people in the Middle East and Asia built earthen mounds across rivers and along their edges to prevent or minimize flooding. Such artificial embankments helped hold Chinese rivers in check for centuries. Today, engineering works remain one of the main ways in which people try to control floods. Engineers build barriers such as levees, dikes, and dams to hold back floodwater, and they create new channels to divert floodwater away from populated areas. They also improve river channels to make them less prone to flooding. Another important approach to flood control is the conservation of wetlands, forests, and grasslands, which can absorb large amounts of water and help stop the flow of runoff from storms.

TYPES OF FLOODS

RIVER FLOODS

If a river receives an unusually large amount of water—from heavy rains, rapid snow or ice melt, or a levee or dam failure—it may overflow its banks, causing flooding. Some of the deadliest floods have happened when China's Huang He (Yellow River) surpassed its banks. The silt that gives the river its yellow tint and name can build up along the riverbed, making the lower reaches of the river prone to disastrous flooding.

COASTAL FLOODS

Coastal floods occur when a tsunami or severe storm forces the sea to rush inland. Underwater earthquakes and volcanic eruptions can create huge ocean waves called tsunamis that inundate coasts far and near. The torrential rains and storm surge that often accompany tropical cyclones can cause major coastal flooding.

New Orleans, Louisiana, after Hurricane Katrina

FLASH FLOODS

Flash floods are usually caused by sudden, unexpected torrents of rain. Flash floods often occur in hilly country or around dry riverbeds. A flash flood can fill a completely dry riverbed in minutes. The fast-moving water can sweep away anything in its path, including bridges, houses, and cars. The collapse of a dam can also trigger a destructive flash flood, such as the Johnstown, Pennsylvania, flood of May 1889. Because of their suddenness, flash floods can be especially deadly.

MONSOONS

A monsoon is a major wind system that seasonally reverses its direction. Monsoon winds typically bring wet summers and dry winters to the regions where they blow. The largest monsoon regions are in South Asia and West Africa, but monsoons also affect northern Australia. Most summer monsoons come from the west, and most winter monsoons come from the east. In South Asia, the summer monsoon blows from the southwest to the northeast—from the Indian Ocean to India. During the wet season, moist air is cooled as it blows over rising land, letting abundant rain fall on mountain ranges. This situation makes Cherrapunji, India, just north of Bangladesh, one of the rainiest places in the world with an average annual rainfall of 450 inches (1,143 centimeters), most of which falls in six months.

Monsoons can be both a blessing and a curse. Summer monsoons bring lots of rain to India, Bangladesh, Sri Lanka, Pakistan, and Myanmar. Farmers in these areas depend on monsoon rains to water their crops. But excessive monsoon rains can also cause dangerous flooding and damage crops.

WHAT CAUSES MONSOONS?

WHICH MONSOON SEASON?

SUMMER

WINTER

PAKISTAN MONSOON FLOODS OF 2010

In 2010, Pakistan experienced some of the worst floods in the nation's history after the Indus River burst its banks. Record monsoon rains began to fall in Pakistan's mountainous northwest region around July 22, causing flash floods in three provinces. The unprecedented amount of rainwater swept away roads and bridges and inundated large areas of land. As the floodwaters surged downriver in August, rain continued to fall in the northwest. The consequences of the 2010 floods continued long after the monsoon season had passed and the Indus receded. The flooding, which affected approximately 20 million people, destroyed homes, crops, and infrastructure and left millions vulnerable to malnutrition and disease.

Some of Earth's rainiest places are in the path of the Indian monsoon. In which place did 98.15 inches (249.3 centimeters) of rain fall during a 2-day period in June 1995, setting the record for greatest 48-hour rainfall?

- **Chittagong, Bangladesh**
- **Lahore, Pakistan**
- **Cherrapunji, India**

WHAT'S THE MONSOON CUP?

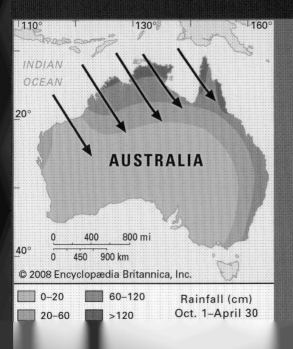

INDIAN OCEAN

AUSTRALIA

| 0 | 400 | 800 mi |
| 0 | 450 | 900 km |

© 2008 Encyclopædia Britannica, Inc.

| | 0–20 | | 60–120 | Rainfall (cm) |
| | 20–60 | | >120 | Oct. 1–April 30 |

The Malaysian-Australian monsoon affects Southeast Asia and Australia. In Australia, monsoon winds blow southeasterly in the winter (May–September) and northeasterly in the summer (November–April).

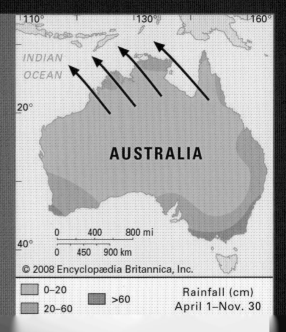

INDIAN OCEAN

AUSTRALIA

| 0 | 400 | 800 mi |
| 0 | 450 | 900 km |

© 2008 Encyclopædia Britannica, Inc.

| | 0–20 | | >60 | Rainfall (cm) |
| | 20–60 | | | April 1–Nov. 30 |

DROUGHTS

Wherever there is a shortage of rain over a long period of time, there is drought. Drought affects plants, animals, and people. It is a serious problem for farmers and for the people who depend on the crops they produce. There are four basic types of drought—unpredictable drought, permanent drought, seasonal drought, and invisible drought. Unpredictable drought is the abnormal failure of rainfall in an area where rainfall is normally adequate. Permanent drought characterizes the driest climates. Deserts receive very little rain all year and are sometimes said to be in a permanent drought. Agriculture is impossible in these places without continuous irrigation. Places that have a rainy season and a dry season have seasonal drought during the dry season. Other places can experience drought at any time. Invisible drought occurs in summer when high temperatures induce high rates of evaporation.

WHICH TYPE OF DROUGHT?

- UNPREDICTABLE DROUGHT
- SEASONAL DROUGHT
- PERMANENT DROUGHT
- INVISIBLE DROUGHT

FAMINE

Severe droughts can last for months or years. When this happens no crops will grow. As a result, many people and animals may die of famine. Severe droughts often force people and animals to move to find water. Some farmers go to places where they think conditions will be better for their crops and animals. Some people give up farming altogether. Beginning in 1968, the Sahel region in western and north-central Africa experienced a long period of drought that destroyed all the crops and more than half of the cattle. By 1973, the loss of human life by starvation and disease was estimated at 100,000. In Somalia in 2010–12, more than 250,000 people—most of them children—died during a severe drought in the area.

With an average annual rainfall of less than 2 inches (5 centimeters), this place is one of the driest in North America and is in permanent drought.

CAN YOU NAME THIS PLACE?

WHAT ARE THE MAIN CAUSES OF DESERTIFICATION?

○ **CHANGES IN CLIMATE**

○ **HUMAN ACTIVITIES**

Which place has the lowest average annual precipitation?

DESERTIFICATION

Desert environments are expanding in many areas of the world. The spread of a desert environment into a nondesert region is a process known as desertification. This process results from a number of factors, including changes in climate and the influence of human activities. Desertification drains an arid or semiarid land of its life-supporting capabilities. The process of desertification is extremely difficult to reverse. Public awareness of desertification increased during the severe drought in the Sahel (1968–73) that accelerated the southward movement of the Sahara. Persistent drought conditions, coupled with substantial growth of both the human and livestock populations in the Sahel, resulted in a gradual desertification of the region.

THE DUST BOWL

The worst drought in modern American history hit the southern Great Plains in the 1930s. The affected region, which included southeastern Colorado, western Kansas, the panhandles of Texas and Oklahoma, and northeastern New Mexico, came to be known as the Dust Bowl. This name was coined to reflect the conditions that occurred after drought, overcultivation, and dust storms hit the region.

Human mistakes made the drought worse. During World War I (1914–18), farmers planted new fields of wheat. Their plows removed millions of acres of native grasslands that had held the soil in place. Cattle grazing on ranches removed more grass. The loss of the grass cover loosened the soil. Winds blew it away in giant dust storms that blackened the sky.

The U.S. government helped the Dust Bowl area recover. Government programs planted grass and trees as windbreaks. A government agency taught farmers better farming methods. Near the end of the 1930s, rainfall finally increased. By the early 1940s the fields were productive again.

TRUE OR FALSE?

T F

SOME FARM FIELDS IN THE DUST BOWL REGION LOST UP TO 12 INCHES (30 CENTIMETERS) OF VITAL TOPSOIL DURING THIS PERIOD.

WHAT WERE DUST STORMS SOMETIMES CALLED DURING THIS ERA?

CONTOUR FARMING

Extreme heat made the Dust Bowl drought worse. In 1936, parts of Texas reached what temperature?

113° F (45° C)

117° F (47° C)

120° F (49° C)

WILDFIRES

Wildfires, also known as wildland fires, forest fires, or bushfires, are uncontrolled fires in a forest, grassland, or brushland. Fire danger in a wildland setting varies with weather conditions. Drought, heat, and wind participate in drying out the timber or other fuel, making it easier to ignite. Once a fire is burning, drought, heat, and wind all increase its intensity.

FIRE TRIANGLE

In order to burn, a wildfire must have fuel, oxygen, and heat. These three elements make up the fire triangle. Fuel is anything that burns, including dried grass, fallen leaves, trees, and even homes. Air provides the oxygen a fire needs. And lightning, campfires, cigarettes, or hot winds can provide enough heat to spark a wildfire. Firefighters put out fires by removing at least one of the three fire ingredients. They take fuel away from a wildfire by clearing away trees and bushes in the path of the fire. They take oxygen away from a grease fire by smothering it with foam from a fire extinguisher. They reduce the heat of a burning building by spraying water over it.

OXYGEN

FUEL

HEAT

WHICH WAY DO WILDFIRES SPREAD MORE QUICKLY?

UPHILL   DOWNHILL

FIRE FIGURES

90 75
1,000,000
173 6,800
115 3

WHAT'S A CROWN FIRE?

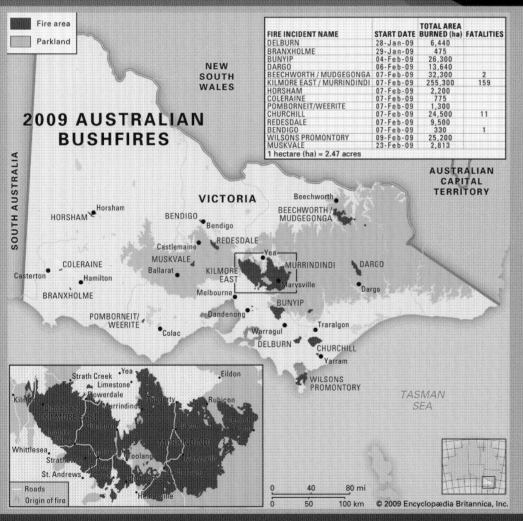

2009 AUSTRALIAN BUSHFIRES

Fire area
Parkland

NEW SOUTH WALES

SOUTH AUSTRALIA

VICTORIA

Horsham
HORSHAM
BENDIGO
Bendigo
Beechworth
BEECHWORTH / MUDGEGONGA
REDESDALE
Castlemaine
MUSKVALE
COLERAINE
Ballarat
KILMORE EAST
MURRINDINDI
DARGO
Casterton
Hamilton
Yea
Marysville
Dargo
BRANXHOLME
Melbourne
BUNYIP
POMBORNEIT/WEERITE
Dandenong
Traralgon
Colac
Warragul
DELBURN
CHURCHILL
Yarram
WILSONS PROMONTORY

AUSTRALIAN CAPITAL TERRITORY

TASMAN SEA

Strath Creek
Yea
Eildon
Limestone
Flowerdale
Kilmore
Clonbinane
KILMORE EAST
Murrindindi
Taggerty
Rubicon
Buxton
Whittlesea
MURRINDINDI
Strathewen
Toolangi
Marysville
St. Andrews
Healesville

Roads
Origin of fire

0   40   80 mi
0   50   100 km
© 2009 Encyclopædia Britannica, Inc.

FIRE INCIDENT NAME	START DATE	TOTAL AREA BURNED (ha)	FATALITIES
DELBURN	28-Jan-09	6,440	
BRANXHOLME	29-Jan-09	475	
BUNYIP	04-Feb-09	26,300	
DARGO	06-Feb-09	13,640	
BEECHWORTH / MUDGEGONGA	07-Feb-09	32,300	2
KILMORE EAST / MURRINDINDI	07-Feb-09	255,300	159
HORSHAM	07-Feb-09	2,200	
COLERAINE	07-Feb-09	775	
POMBORNEIT/WEERITE	07-Feb-09	1,300	
CHURCHILL	07-Feb-09	24,500	11
REDESDALE	07-Feb-09	9,500	
BENDIGO	07-Feb-09	330	1
WILSONS PROMONTORY	09-Feb-09	25,200	
MUSKVALE	23-Feb-09	2,813	

1 hectare (ha) = 2.47 acres

AUSTRALIA BUSHFIRES OF 2009

The Australia bushfires of 2009 were a series of fires that killed 173 people, injured 500, and destroyed numerous homes in the Australian state of Victoria on February 7, 2009, a day later dubbed "Black Saturday." With its abundant forests and hot, dry climate, Australia has often suffered from deadly bushfires, most notably the 1939 "Black Friday" blaze in Victoria, in which 71 people were killed, and the 1983 "Ash Wednesday" fires in Victoria and South Australia, where 75 people perished.

WHAT'S THE DIFFERENCE BETWEEN FLASH FUELS AND GREEN FUELS?

- FLASH FUELS
- GREEN FUELS

RING OF FIRE

The Ring of Fire is a seismically active belt of volcanoes and tectonic plate boundaries that stretches 24,900 miles (40,000 kilometers) around the Pacific Ocean. Most of the world's strongest earthquakes and about three-fourths of the world's volcanic eruptions occur within the Ring of Fire. Major volcanic events that have occurred there include the eruptions of Mount Tambora (1815), Krakatoa (1883), Mount Saint Helens (1980), Mount Ruiz (1985), and Mount Pinatubo (1991). The Ring of Fire has been the setting for several of the largest earthquakes in recorded history, including the Chile earthquakes of 1960 and 2010, the Alaska earthquake of 1964, and the Japan earthquake of 2011, as well as the earthquake that produced the devastating Indian Ocean tsunami of 2004.

FIND IT!

EURASIAN PLATE

ASIA

INDIAN PLATE

PHILIPPINE PLATE

SENDAI, JAPAN

P A
P

R I

R I N G O

CAPRICORN PLATE

KRAKATOA, INDONESIA

INDIAN OCEAN

AUSTRALIA

AUSTRALIAN PLATE

TECTONIC PLATES

The Ring of Fire contains several **tectonic plates**—including the vast Pacific Plate and the smaller Philippine, Juan de Fuca, Cocos, and Nazca plates. As the plates grind into each other, they cause earthquakes and volcanoes.

HOW MUCH DO THE PLATES MOVE EACH YEAR?

2–4 INCHES (5–10 CENTIMETERS)

4–6 INCHES (10–15 CENTIMETERS)

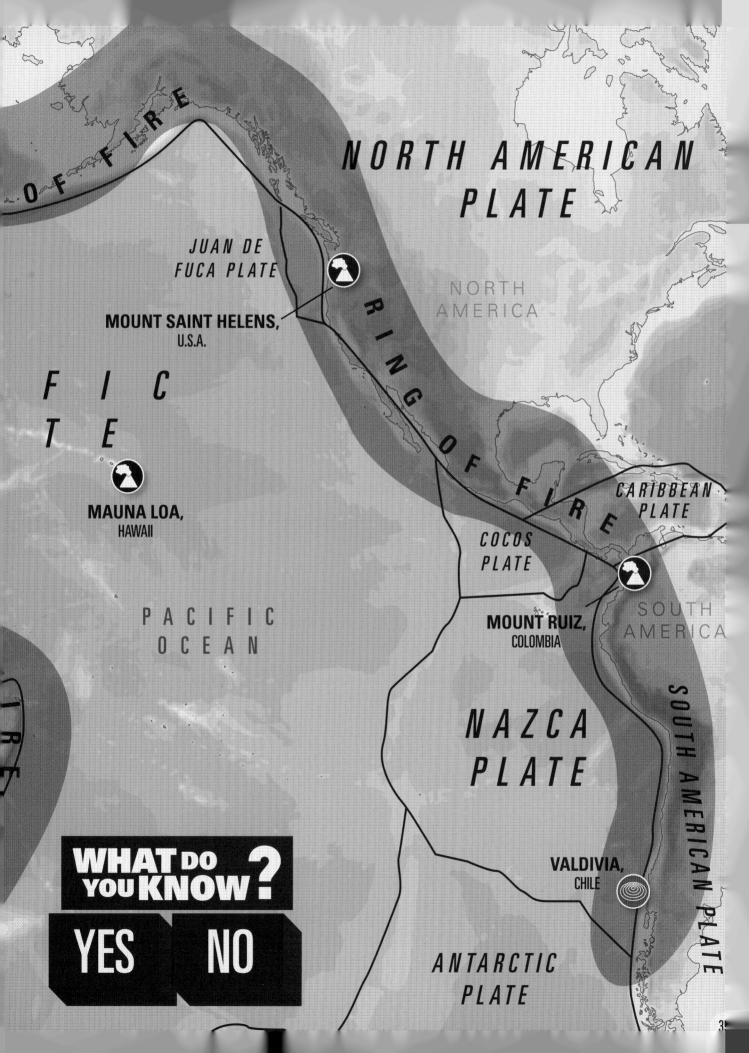

NORTH AMERICAN PLATE

JUAN DE FUCA PLATE

MOUNT SAINT HELENS, U.S.A.

NORTH AMERICA

RING OF FIRE

F I C
T E

MAUNA LOA, HAWAII

PACIFIC OCEAN

CARIBBEAN PLATE

COCOS PLATE

MOUNT RUIZ, COLOMBIA

SOUTH AMERICA

NAZCA PLATE

SOUTH AMERICAN PLATE

VALDIVIA, CHILE

ANTARCTIC PLATE

WHAT DO YOU KNOW?

YES   NO

VOLCANOES

When a volcano erupts, hot gases and melted rock from deep within Earth find their way up to the surface. This material may flow slowly out of a fissure, or crack, in the ground, or it may explode suddenly into the air.

TRUE OR FALSE?

T F

HOW HOT IS LAVA?

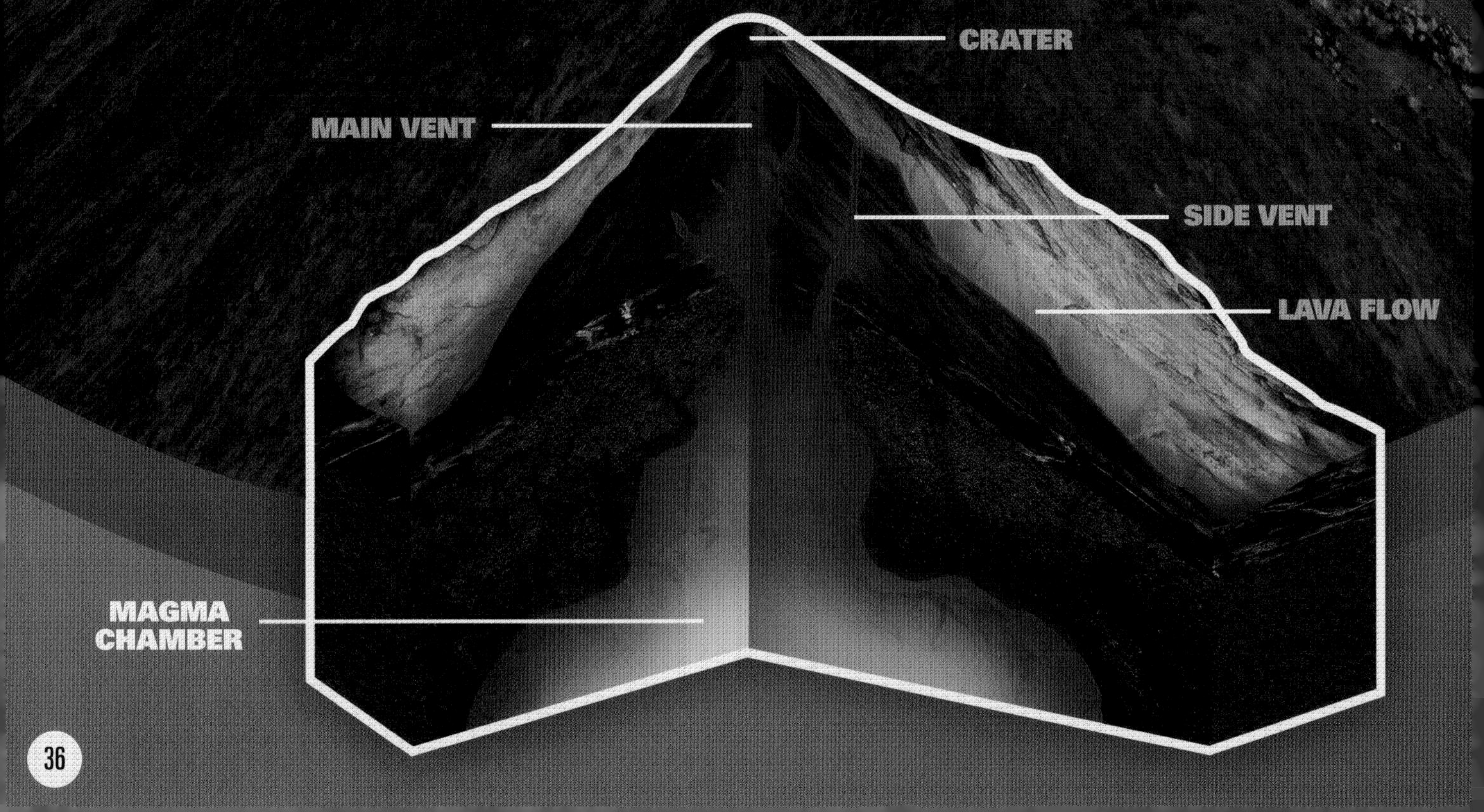

CRATER

MAIN VENT

SIDE VENT

LAVA FLOW

MAGMA CHAMBER

WHAT'S THE DIFFERENCE BETWEEN MAGMA AND LAVA?

HOW *FAST* DOES LAVA MOVE?

VOLCANIC LANDFORMS

Volcanoes are usually classified by shape and size. These are determined by such factors as the volume and type of volcanic material ejected, the sequence and variety of eruptions, and the environment. Among the most common types are shield volcanoes and stratovolcanoes.

CALDERAS

Sometimes the top of a volcano collapses and forms a pit called a caldera. A caldera is larger than a crater. Some calderas fill up with water to form lakes. A **somma volcano** forms when a new volcanic cone partially fills a caldera.

SHIELD VOLCANOES

Shield volcanoes are dome-shaped mountains built by lava flows. They are not as steep as stratovolcanoes, though they can be quite large. Some shield volcanoes that erupt under the sea grow high enough to create islands.

COMPLEX VOLCANOES

A complex volcano has more than one vent. A volcano can have more than one vent when two cones overlap one another. Or a volcano can form new vents during an explosion.

? WHICH TYPE?

HOT SPRINGS, GEYSERS, AND FUMAROLES

Hot springs, geysers, and fumaroles are other types of volcanic activity. They happen in places where magma heats underground water. A **hot spring** is a place where warm water comes up through the ground. A **geyser** is a kind of hot spring that shoots water and steam into the air. A **fumarole** is a vent that releases gas and steam.

STRATOVOLCANOES

Stratovolcanoes, also called composite volcanoes, are mountains shaped like cones. They have a narrow top with steep sides and a wide bottom. A crater, or bowl-shaped pit, usually lies at the top. Stratovolcanoes are made up of layers of hardened lava and ash. Thousands of eruptions left these layers over millions of years.

EPIC ERUPTIONS

KRAKATOA

The volcano Krakatoa (also spelled Krakatau) is located on an island in the Sunda Strait between Java and Sumatra, Indonesia. On the afternoon of August 26, 1883, the first of a series of increasingly violent explosions occurred. A black cloud of ash rose 17 miles (27 kilometers) above Krakatoa. On the morning of the next day, tremendous explosions were heard 2,200 miles (3,540 kilometers) away in Australia. Destructive tsunami waves reached as far away as Hawaii and South America. The greatest wave reached a height of 120 feet (36 meters) and took 36,000 lives in the coastal towns of nearby Java and Sumatra.

MOUNT PELÉE

Mount Pelée is an active volcanic mountain on the Caribbean island of Martinique. Minor eruptions occurred in 1792 and 1851, but on May 8, 1902, a major eruption occurred. Although very little lava flowed, an unstoppable black cloud of hot gases and ash engulfed the port city of Saint-Pierre, killing most of its 29,000 inhabitants.

WHERE DOES THE WORD *VOLCANO* COME FROM?

MOUNT TAMBORA

Mount Tambora, in what is now Indonesia, erupted violently in April 1815. The eruption and tsunamis that followed caused the deaths of at least 10,000 islanders and destroyed the homes of 35,000 more. Some 80,000 people in the region eventually died from starvation and disease related to the event. Many volcanologists regard the eruption as the largest in recorded history. It released so much ash into the air that it blocked out large amounts of sunlight. Temperatures around the world dropped for months afterward, making 1816 the "year without a summer."

MOUNT PINATUBO

Mount Pinatubo is a volcano located about 55 miles (90 kilometers) northwest of Manila, the capital of the Philippines, and rose to a height of about 4,800 feet (1,460 meters) prior to its eruption in the late 20th century. When it erupted in 1991 for the first time in 600 years, Mount Pinatubo caused widespread devastation. After two months of small explosions, a series of major explosions began on June 12. These explosions reached a peak on June 14–16, producing a column of ash and smoke more than 19 miles (30 kilometers) high, with rock debris falling the same distance from the volcano. The resulting heavy ashfalls left about 100,000 people homeless, forced thousands more to flee the area, and caused 300 deaths.

MOUNT ETNA

MOUNT KILAUEA

MOUNT PELÉE

MOUNT SAINT HELENS

MOUNT TAMBORA

MOUNT VESUVIUS

MOUNT VESUVIUS

Mount Vesuvius is an active volcano in southern Italy. Its fiery eruptions have claimed a high toll in lives and property through the centuries, but the mountainside and surrounding area remain the home of more than two million people. The most famous eruption of Vesuvius occurred in AD 79, when lava and ashes buried the towns of Pompeii, Herculaneum, and Stabiae. Excavations have uncovered parts of the cities. Since that disaster, nearly 50 eruptions of varying intensity have been reported. An eruption in 1631 buried villages and blew ashes as far as 150 miles (240 kilometers). Despite the warnings of earthquakes for many months before the eruption, people remained in the area and more than 3,000 were killed.

MOUNT ETNA

Mount Etna, which is located on the coast of Sicily, is the highest active volcano in Europe. More than 135 eruptions have been recorded there. An eruption in AD 1169 killed 15,000 people in the town of Catania at the volcano's base. An eruption in 1669 lasted from March 11 through July 15 and killed some 20,000 people. The lava flow destroyed a dozen villages and submerged the western part of Catania. Workers attempted to turn the lava stream away from Catania by digging a trench above the village. This attempt is recognized as the first in history to divert a lava stream. In 1983, an eruption lasted almost four months. Authorities exploded dynamite in an attempt to divert lava flow.

WHICH TYPE?

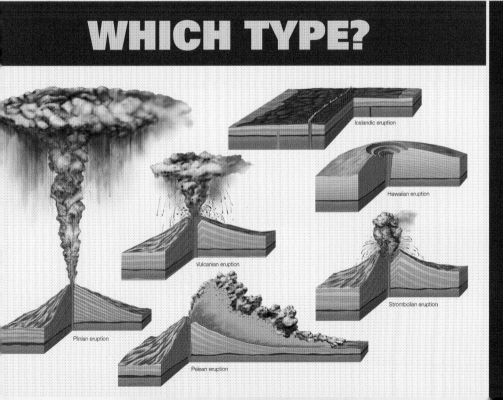

Icelandic eruption

Hawaiian eruption

Vulcanian eruption

Strombolian eruption

Plinian eruption

Pelean eruption

SOUFRIÈRE

Soufrière is an active volcano on the island of Saint Vincent in the Caribbean Sea. The volcano rises to peaks of 3,864 feet (1,178 meters) and 4,048 feet (1,234 meters) north of the crater. It erupted violently in 1812 and again in 1902, when it seriously damaged the northern part of the island and killed some 1,600 people. A series of mild eruptions in 1971–72 caused no damage, but eruptions in April 1979 forced authorities to evacuate residents of communities surrounding the foothills of the volcano. There was no loss of life, but agriculture suffered considerably.

EARTHQUAKES

The sudden shaking of the ground that occurs when masses of rock change position below Earth's surface is called an earthquake. The shifting masses send out shock waves that may be powerful enough to alter the surface, thrusting up cliffs and opening great cracks in the ground. Earthquakes occur almost continuously. Fortunately, only sensitive instruments called seismographs can detect most of them. Others are felt as small tremors. Some of the rest, however, cause major catastrophes. They produce such tragic and dramatic effects as destroyed cities, broken dams, landslides, giant sea waves called tsunamis, and volcanic eruptions.

SAN ANDREAS FAULT

WHAT IS THE STUDY OF EARTHQUAKES CALLED?

NUMBER MATCH

Touch a number on the left. Then touch the matching description on the right.

800 — levels of earthquake strength in Modified Mercalli Intensity Scale

50,000 — approximate number of earthquakes big enough to produce substantial damage each year

100 — average number of people that die each year as a result of earthquakes

12 — annual number of earthquakes large enough to be noticed without instruments

10,000 — length of San Andreas Fault in miles

SHOCK WAVES

The shifting rock in an earthquake causes shock waves—called seismic waves—to spread through the rock in all directions. In a great earthquake, people thousands of miles away from the center may feel shocks. There are two broad classes of seismic waves—body waves and surface waves.

BODY WAVES

Body waves travel within the body of Earth. They include P, or primary, waves and S, or secondary, waves.

• **P WAVES**   • **S WAVES**

SURFACE WAVES

After both P and S waves have moved through the body of Earth, they are followed by two types of surface waves, Love and Rayleigh waves, which travel along Earth's surface.

• **LOVE WAVES**   • **RAYLEIGH WAVES**

BODY WAVES VS. SURFACE WAVES

BODY WAVES

SURFACE WAVES

EFFECTS OF EARTHQUAKES

Earthquakes often cause dramatic changes at Earth's surface. In addition to the ground movements, other surface effects include damage to infrastructure, landslides, tsunamis, and fires.

DAMAGE TO STRUCTURES

LANDSLIDES

TSUNAMIS

FIRES

DO NATURAL FORCES CAUSE ALL EARTHQUAKES?

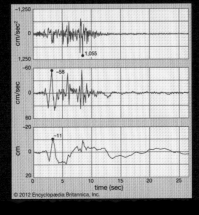

© 2012 Encyclopædia Britannica, Inc.

SEISMOGRAPHS

A seismograph records the pattern of shock waves caused by an earthquake. Seismographs are equipped with electromagnetic sensors that translate ground motions into electrical changes, which are processed and recorded by the instrument. A record produced by a seismograph on a display screen or paper printout is called a seismogram.

QUAKE QUIZ

NOTABLE QUAKES

HAITI EARTHQUAKE OF 2010

On January 12, 2010, at 4:53 p.m., a large earthquake struck some 15 miles (25 kilometers) southwest of the Haitian capital of Port-au-Prince. The initial shock registered a magnitude of 7.0 and was soon followed by two aftershocks of magnitudes 5.9 and 5.5. More aftershocks occurred in the following days, including another one of magnitude 5.9 that struck on January 20 at Petit Goâve, a town some 35 miles (55 kilometers) west of Port-au-Prince. Haiti had not been hit by an earthquake of such enormity since the 18th century, the closest in force being a 1984 shock of magnitude 6.9.

CHILE EARTHQUAKE OF 1960

The largest earthquake recorded in the 20th century originated off the coast of southern Chile on May 22, 1960. The quake caused substantial damage and loss of life both in that country and—as a result of the tsunamis that it generated—in distant Pacific coastal areas. The earthquake hit at 7:11 p.m. approximately 100 miles (160 kilometers) off the coast of Chile, parallel to the city of Valdivia. The shock is generally agreed to have had a magnitude of 9.5, though some studies alternately proposed that it might have been 9.4 or 9.6. A series of foreshocks the previous day had warned of the incipient disaster; one, of magnitude 7.9, caused major destruction in Concepción.

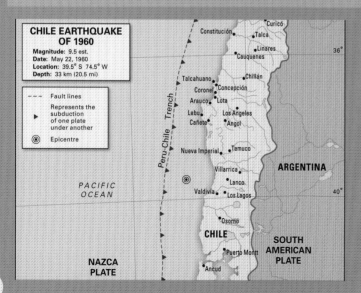

CHILE EARTHQUAKE OF 1960
Magnitude: 9.5 est.
Date: May 22, 1960
Location: 39.5° S 74.5° W
Depth: 33 km (20.5 mi)

– – – Fault lines
▶ Represents the subduction of one plate under another
◎ Epicentre

PACIFIC OCEAN

Peru-Chile Trench

Constitución • Curicó • Talca
• Linares
Cauquenes
Talcahuano • Chillán
Coronel • Concepción
Arauco • Lota
Lebu • Los Angeles
Cañete • Angol
Nueva Imperial • Temuco
Villarrica
• Lanco
Valdivia • Los Lagos
• Osorno
CHILE
• Puerto Montt
• Ancud

ARGENTINA

SOUTH AMERICAN PLATE

NAZCA PLATE

36°
40°

SAN FRANCISCO EARTHQUAKE OF 1906

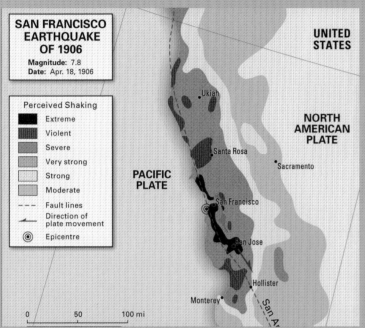

SAN FRANCISCO EARTHQUAKE OF 1906
Magnitude: 7.8
Date: Apr. 18, 1906

Perceived Shaking
- Extreme
- Violent
- Severe
- Very strong
- Strong
- Moderate
- Fault lines
- Direction of plate movement
- Epicentre

UNITED STATES

NORTH AMERICAN PLATE

PACIFIC PLATE

Ukiah
Santa Rosa
Sacramento
San Francisco
San Jose
Hollister
Monterey

San A...

0   50   100 mi

On April 18, 1906, at 5:12 a.m., a major earthquake struck off the northern California coast. The San Andreas Fault slipped along a segment about 270 miles (430 kilometers) long, extending from San Juan Bautista in San Benito County to Humboldt County. The shaking was felt from Los Angeles in the south to Coos Bay, Oregon, in the north. Damage was severe in San Francisco and in other towns situated near the fault, including San Jose, Salinas, and Santa Rosa. At least 700 people were killed in the magnitude-7.8 quake. In San Francisco, the earthquake started a fire that destroyed the central business district.

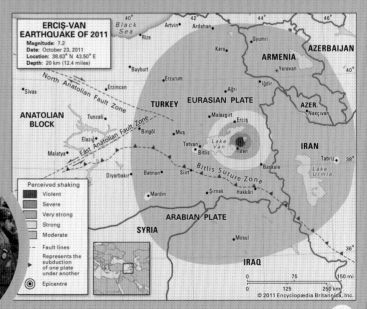

WHAT'S AN AFTERSHOCK?

ERCIŞ-VAN EARTHQUAKE OF 2011

The Erciş-Van Earthquake of 2011 struck near the cities of Erciş and Van in eastern Turkey on October 23. More than 570 people were killed, and thousands of structures in Erciş, Van, and other nearby towns were destroyed. The earthquake was felt as far away as Jordan and southern Russia. The initial shock, which registered a moment magnitude of 7.2, struck at 1:41 p.m. local time. Its epicenter was about 10 miles (16 kilometers) northeast of Van. A magnitude-6.0 aftershock, which was one of more than 200 such events that were recorded in eastern Turkey within the first 24 hours after the earthquake, struck at 11:45 p.m. the same day some 15.5 miles (25 kilometers) from the epicenter of the initial earthquake.

ERCIŞ-VAN EARTHQUAKE OF 2011
Magnitude: 7.2
Date: October 23, 2011
Location: 38.63° N 43.50° E
Depth: 20 km (12.4 miles)

Black Sea
Artvin Ardahan
Rize
Kars
Gyumri
ARMENIA
AZERBAIJAN
Bayburt
Erzurum
Erzincan
Yerevan
Ağrı
Iğdir
North Anatolian Fault Zone
Sivas
TURKEY
EURASIAN PLATE
AZER.
Naxçivan
ANATOLIAN BLOCK
Tunceli
Malazgirt
Erciş
Bingöl
Muş
Elazığ
Tatvan
Lake Van
Van
IRAN
Malatya
Bitlis
Tabriz
East Anatolian Fault Zone
Başkale
Lake Urmia
Diyarbakır
Batman
Siirt
Bitlis Suture Zone
Perceived shaking
- Violent
- Severe
- Very strong
- Strong
- Moderate
- Fault lines
- Represents the subduction of one plate under another
- Epicentre
Mardin
Şırnak
Hakkâri
ARABIAN PLATE
SYRIA
Mosul
IRAQ

0   75   150 mi
0   125   250 km
© 2011 Encyclopædia Britannica, Inc.

TSUNAMIS

Natural disasters, both on land and under the ocean, may cause deadly ocean waves called tsunamis. Tsunamis can challenge a jet airplane for speed and can beat a three-story building for height. After an earthquake, volcanic eruption, or other cause triggers a tsunami, a series of waves spreads over the ocean surface in ever-widening circles. By the time a tsunami reaches shore, it has gained tremendous size and power. Tsunamis can wipe out entire coastal communities in minutes.

THE WORD TSUNAMI IS A JAPANESE WORD, REPRESENTED BY TWO CHARACTERS: *TSU,* MEANING "HARBOR," AND *NAMI,* MEANING "WAVE."

TRUE OR FALSE?

T F

earthquake epicentre

sea level

HOW **FAST** CAN TSUNAMIS TRAVEL?

HOW **FAR** CAN TSUNAMIS TRAVEL?

JAPAN'S TRIPLE DISASTER

In March 2011, a powerful underwater earthquake struck off the coast of Japan's main island of Honshu. The magnitude-9.0 quake caused widespread damage on land and triggered a series of large tsunami waves that devastated many coastal areas of Japan, most notably northeastern Honshu. Waves as high as 33 feet (10 meters) struck Sendai and other low-lying coastal regions. In some places, the water reached several miles inland. A few hours later, waves measuring 11 to 12 feet (3.3 to 3.6 meters) were detected in the Hawaiian Islands, and waves measuring about 9 feet (2.7 meters) high washed ashore along the West Coast of the United States.

In the weeks and months following the disaster, another crisis developed in Japan at the Fukushima Daiichi ("Number One") nuclear power plant, located along the Pacific coast about 60 miles (100 kilometers) south of Sendai. Damage caused by the tsunami led to a meltdown in reactor cores at the plant, which caused significant levels of radiation to be released from the facility. The accident forced the evacuation of residents from an area of 18 miles (30 kilometers) around the plant.

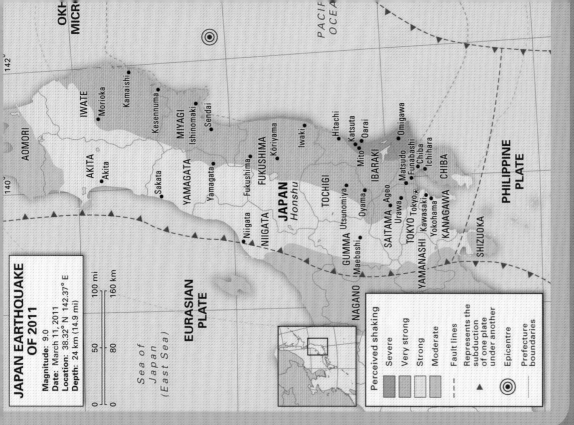

JAPAN EARTHQUAKE OF 2011

Magnitude: 9.0
Date: March 11, 2011
Location: 38.32° N 142.37° E
Depth: 24 km (14.9 mi)

Sea of Japan (East Sea)

EURASIAN PLATE

PHILIPPINE PLATE

JAPAN *Honshu*

PACIFIC OCEAN

OKI- MICR

AOMORI

IWATE

AKITA

YAMAGATA

MIYAGI

NIIGATA

FUKUSHIMA

TOCHIGI

GUMMA

NAGANO

SAITAMA

TOKYO

YAMANASHI

KANAGAWA

CHIBA

IBARAKI

SHIZUOKA

Morioka
Kamaishi
Ishinomaki
Sendai
Kesennuma
Akita
Sakata
Yamagata
Niigata
Fukushima
Koriyama
Iwaki
Hitachi
Katsuta
Oarai
Utsunomiya
Mito
Omigawa
Maebashi
Oyama
Ageo
Matsudo
Funabashi
Urawa
Chiba
Kawasaki
Ichihara
Yokohama

Perceived shaking	
	Severe
	Very strong
	Strong
	Moderate

– – – Fault lines
▲ Represents the subduction of one plate under another
◉ Epicentre
— Prefecture boundaries

0   50   100 mi
0   80   160 km

140°
142°

WHERE DO TSUNAMIS TRAVEL FASTER?
● IN DEEP WATER
● IN SHALLOW WATER

WHERE ARE TSUNAMI WAVES HIGHER?
● FAR FROM LAND
● CLOSE TO LAND

INDIAN OCEAN TSUNAMI

In December 2004, a massive undersea earthquake unleashed a catastrophic tsunami in the Indian Ocean. The series of immense ocean waves caused widespread destruction and loss in several countries on the ocean's rim. The earthquake that triggered the tsunami struck off the coast of the Indonesian island of Sumatra on December 26, 2004, at 7:59 a.m. local time. It had a magnitude of 9.1, making it one of the largest earthquakes in recorded history. Two hours later, towering waves hit the eastern coasts of India and Sri Lanka, some 750 miles (1,200 kilometers) away. Within seven hours of the quake, waves washed ashore in East Africa, more than 1,800 miles (3,000 kilometers) away on the other side of the Indian Ocean. Some locations reported that the waves had reached a height of 30 feet (9 meters) or more when they hit the shoreline. The tsunami killed at least 225,000 people across a dozen countries, with Indonesia, Sri Lanka, India, Maldives, and Thailand sustaining massive damage. Indonesian officials estimated that the death toll there alone exceeded 200,000.

LANDSLIDES

A landslide is a large mass of rock, debris, earth, or soil that moves down a slope. Landslides occur when a layer of earth or rocks separates from the layer below it. The force of gravity pulls the loose layer downward. Landslides differ in their type, speed, extent, and destructiveness. They can bury or sweep away everything in their path.

HOW FAST CAN LANDSLIDES TRAVEL?

VOCAB CHALLENGE

AVALANCHE	BULGING
LAHAR	SUBMARINE LANDSLIDE
CREEP	ROCKFALL
EARTHFLOW	TOPPLING

CAUSES

Landslides occur when the rock, earth, or other material on a slope becomes too weak to resist the force of gravity. Often, this results from the slope's having become too steep. Human modification of the landscape and erosion by water—such as from rain, melting snow, rivers, ocean waves, or rising groundwater—can steepen the slope. Intense rainfall and flooding can also loosen the surface material and overload the slope, initiating a landslide. Heavy or sustained rainfall or rapidly melting snow and ice can cause a mudflow. Earthquakes, volcanic eruptions, and human activities such as excavation or changing water-drainage patterns can also cause a landslide. An underwater earthquake can trigger an underwater, or submarine, landslide, which in turn can set off a tsunami. Wildfires can create conditions favorable to landslides, in part by destroying the vegetation that had anchored the soil on a slope.

TYPES OF LANDSLIDES

SLIDES

Slides involve the displacement of material that moves downward as a single unit. The sliding can extend downward and outward along a broadly flat surface (a translational slide), or it can be rotational along a concave (bowl-shaped) surface (a slump).

FLOWS

There are five broad categories of flows.

DEBRIS FLOW   **MUDFLOW**

DEBRIS AVALANCHE   **CREEP**

EARTHFLOW

SPREADS

A spread is the complex lateral movement of relatively consistent earth materials resting on a weaker underlying base layer that is subject to liquefaction. The liquefaction may be caused by water saturation or earthquake shock. When firm blocks of material settle into the weaker underlying layer, the unstable base layer causes the material to slowly move downward. The spread frequently extends long distances.

TOPPLES

Rotation of a mass of rock, debris, or earth outward from a steep slope face is called toppling. This type of movement can subsequently cause the mass to fall or slide.

FALLS

Falls are the sudden separation of geologic materials such as rocks from steep slopes or cliffs. A rockfall involves large rocks falling from the top of a slope or a cliff.

AVALANCHES

An avalanche is the sudden downward movement of snow or other material.

VENEZUELA MUDSLIDES OF 1999

Over the course of 10 days in December 1999, torrential rains inundated the mountainous regions of Venezuela, causing deadly mudslides that devastated the state of Vargas and other areas in the northern part of the country. The coastal regions were hardest hit, with a 60-mile (100-kilometer) stretch of coastline being wiped out. December 16 saw the most destruction, due to particularly heavy rains throughout the previous day and evening. Flooding caused additional damage and misery. An estimated 190,000 people were evacuated, but thousands of others, likely between 10,000 and 30,000, were killed.

SICHUAN MUDSLIDES OF 2008

The magnitude-7.9 earthquake that occurred in the mountainous central region of Sichuan province in southwestern China on May 12, 2008, triggered devastating mudslides. Some 200 relief workers were reported to have died in mudslides in the affected area, where damming of rivers and lakes by rocks, mud, and earthquake debris made flooding a major threat until workers could open channels to drain the impounded water.

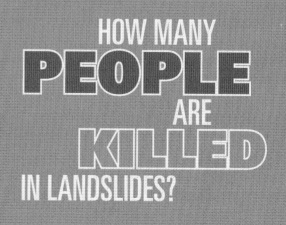

HOW MANY **PEOPLE** ARE KILLED IN LANDSLIDES?

AVALANCHES

An avalanche is a large mass of snow moving rapidly down a mountain slope. The snow breaks loose from its surroundings and quickly collects more snow as it plunges downslope. Avalanches can also be formed of rock, earth, or soil.

Certain conditions of the terrain, the weather, and the snowpack make avalanches more or less likely. The stability of the layers that make up the snowpack is a key factor. Once the snow is on the ground, changes in temperature, precipitation, and other conditions cause the ice crystals to undergo physical changes that differentiate the layers deeper in the snowpack from those on top. These changes can weaken a layer below a block of snow and thereby help set up a slab avalanche.

For an avalanche to occur, there also needs to be a trigger, which supplies sufficient force to start the slide. Common triggers include new deposits of snow and the weight of skiers, snowmobilers, or snowboarders. Explosions and very loud sonic booms can also set off an avalanche.

TYPES OF AVALANCHES

- ROCK AVALANCHES
- ICE AVALANCHES
- DEBRIS AVALANCHES
- SNOW AVALANCHES

MORE OR LESS LIKELY ?

MORE | LESS

TIROL AVALANCHES OF 1916

In World War I, during fighting in the Alps on the Austrian-Italian front in December 1916, a series of massive avalanches killed as many as 10,000 troops in the mountainous Tirol region. The winter of 1915–16 in the Alpine region was one the snowiest on record, with more than 40 feet (12 meters) of snow falling in some areas. The heavy accumulation, combined with the detonation of explosives planted underneath enemy positions, resulted in huge snowslides that took out thousands of troops from each side. Many soldiers remain buried and frozen in the snow; some bodies were recovered as many as 80 years later.

SPEED LIMIT 80

The sliding snow of an avalanche can reach speeds of 80 miles (130 kilometers) per hour!

CAN YELLING TRIGGER AN AVALANCHE?

HOW A SLAB AVALANCHE OCCURS

WHAT IS SLUFFING?

PREDICTION AND PREVENTION

In areas prone to avalanches, a variety of methods are used to predict and prevent the slides. Avalanche forecasters collect field data and use their knowledge of the affected terrain and the past and current weather and snowpack conditions to predict when and where avalanches are most likely to occur. A common method of avalanche control consists of detonating explosives in the upper reaches of avalanche zones, which intentionally causes the snow to slide down before large amounts can pile up. In some areas, devices such as avalanche rakes (large reinforced fences) are used on slopes to hold snow in place. Dams or wedges may be used at the base of the slope to stop, split, or deflect the snow in an avalanche.

A sinkhole is a topographic depression formed as underlying limestone bedrock is dissolved by groundwater. It is considered the most fundamental structure of karst topography. Sinkholes vary greatly in area and depth and may be very large. There are two main varieties, one caused by the collapse of the roof of a cavern, the other by the gradual dissolving of rock under a soil mantle. Collapsed sinkholes generally have steep rock sides and may receive streams that then flow underground. The soil-mantled sinkhole is generally shallower than the collapsed sinkhole and receives local drainage; it may become clogged with clay and hold a small lake. Some sinkholes, formed at low sea-level stages during the Pleistocene epoch, are now half-drowned and are known as cenotes.

SINKHOLES

FIND IT!

Karst terrain is usually characterized by barren, rocky ground, sinkholes, caves, underground rivers, and the absence of surface streams and lakes. It results when circulating groundwater dissolves massive soluble limestone. Karst terrain was originally named after a region with similar features in Europe's Balkan Peninsula. These are regions of mostly limestone, dolomite, gypsum, or salt bedrock and abundant groundwater. Karsts are found in widely scattered sections of the world, including the Causses of France; the Kwangsi area of China; the Yucatán Peninsula; and the Midwest, Kentucky, and Florida in the United States.

? WHICH TYPE?

TYPES OF SINKHOLES

- **SOLUTION SINKHOLES**
- **COLLAPSE SINKHOLES**
- **COVER COLLAPSE AND COVER SUBSIDENCE SINKHOLES**
- **POLJES**

In 1981, a cover collapse sinkhole formed in Winter Park, Florida, and swallowed a private home, a municipal swimming pool, and part of a repair shop in a relatively small amount of time.

CENOTES

Steep-walled sinkholes known as cenotes are common in the Yucatán Peninsula. A major source of water in modern and ancient Yucatán, cenotes form when a limestone surface collapses, exposing water underneath.

Naturally occurring sinkholes, which are common in karst terrain, may be triggered by weather events such as heavy rainfall or by drought followed by heavy rain. A significant percentage of sinkholes, however, are associated, either directly or indirectly, with human activity. In some cases excessive withdrawals of groundwater for irrigation have lowered water levels and thereby allowed saturated soil to wash down into caves and conduits in the underlying bedrock, which can trigger sinkhole formation. In addition, cover collapse sinkholes have formed along roads or other areas where water is repeatedly released onto the ground, washing soil into underlying bedrock cavities and creating soil caves that can collapse.

OUT OF THIS WORLD

Earth isn't the only planet with wild weather. Gas giants Saturn, Jupiter, and Neptune have enormous cyclonic storms that can last for years. Mars has dust storms and dust devils.

WHICH PLANET?

SATURN

Like Jupiter, Saturn has alternating brighter and darker bands of clouds being pushed by east-west winds. Saturn's strongest winds blow eastward in a band over the Equator from 20° N to 20° S. Maximum wind speeds in this band reach nearly 1,100 miles (1,800 kilometers) per hour. Occasionally, a very large storm erupts on Saturn. These large storms seem to occur at about 30-year intervals, or about once each orbit. This suggests that they may be seasonal features. In addition, there are two huge cyclones apparently fixed in place, one at the North Pole and the other at the South Pole.

JUPITER

Jupiter's clouds appear in colored spots and bright and dark stripes. These markings show the planet's weather patterns. One of the spots is a huge storm called the Great Red Spot. The storm is more than twice as wide as Earth. The Great Red Spot has been continuously observed since 1878 and may even be the same storm that was observed from 1665 to 1713. From its maximum extent of about 30,000 miles (48,000 kilometers) in the late 19th century, the spot has been shrinking.

The Martian volcano Olympus Mons is the largest known volcano in the solar system. Olympus Mons reaches a height of 13 miles (21 kilometers) above the average reference altitude (like sea level on Earth). This makes the volcano more than twice as high as Earth's Mount Everest.

NEPTUNE

Neptune is a stormy world. Voyager 2 detected considerable atmospheric turbulence during its 1989 flyby. An enormous, whirling, Earth-sized storm system called the Great Dark Spot appeared as a dark oval in photographs of the southern hemisphere. A smaller dark spot and a bright, fast-moving cloud called Scooter also appeared. Unlike Jupiter's Great Red Spot, which is at least 300 years old, Neptune's large storm systems do not seem to be as long lasting. The Great Dark Spot did not show up in images made with the Hubble Space Telescope just a couple of years after the Voyager flyby. Another dark spot appeared for a few years in the planet's northern hemisphere in Hubble images taken in the 1990s.

MARS

Rapidly swirling columns of dust, called dust devils, have been seen whirling along the surface of Mars. Dust storms also occur frequently on the planet. They are especially common in the southern hemisphere in spring and summer, when the surface is warmest. About every two or three years, Mars is engulfed by global dust storms. Local temperature differences generate strong winds that lift dust from the surface. The thick dust clouds block the sunlight, gradually causing the surface temperatures to even out and the winds to subside. Some of the atmospheric dust is deposited in a "snowfall" of dust and ice in the polar regions.

PREDICTING THE WEATHER

The weather concerns everyone and has some effect on nearly every human activity. It occurs within the atmosphere, the mixture of gases that completely envelops Earth. Weather is defined as the momentary, day-to-day state of the atmosphere over any place on Earth's surface.

TRUE OR FALSE?

T F

WHAT MAKES UP THE WEATHER?

- WIND
- TEMPERATURE
- ATMOSPHERIC PRESSURE
- HUMIDITY
- CLOUDS
- PRECIPITATION AND STORMS

AIR MASSES AND WEATHER FRONTS

Air that has acquired a fairly uniform temperature and humidity over a large area of Earth's surface is called an air mass. Air masses are of four main types—Arctic (A) or Antarctic (AA), polar (P), tropical (T), and equatorial (E)—depending on where they originate. They are also of either maritime (m) or continental (c) origin. Weather fronts are sharp transition zones between different air masses.

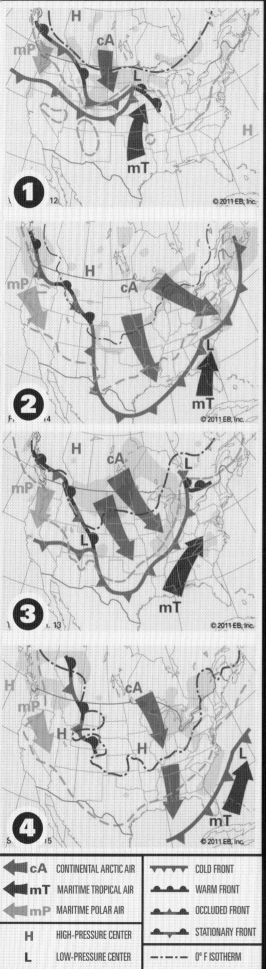

1 12 © 2011 EB, Inc.

2 © 2011 EB, Inc.

3 13 © 2011 EB, Inc.

4 © 2011 EB, Inc.

cA	CONTINENTAL ARCTIC AIR	COLD FRONT	
mT	MARITIME TROPICAL AIR	WARM FRONT	
mP	MARITIME POLAR AIR	OCCLUDED FRONT	
H	HIGH-PRESSURE CENTER	STATIONARY FRONT	
L	LOW-PRESSURE CENTER	0° F ISOTHERM	

WHAT'S THE DIFFERENCE BETWEEN METEOROLOGY AND CLIMATOLOGY?

METEOROLOGY

Meteorology is the scientific study of atmospheric phenomena, particularly variations in the weather and their effects on Earth. This science uses physics and chemistry to unravel the dynamics of Earth's atmosphere in an attempt to understand, predict, and control atmospheric actions. Synoptic and dynamic meteorology are two major branches of meteorology. People who study and predict weather are called meteorologists.

THE TOTAL MASS OF THE ATMOSPHERE IS ESTIMATED TO BE SOME

5.5
QUADRILLION
(55 FOLLOWED BY 14 ZEROS)
TONS
(4.99 QUADRILLION METRIC TONS).

MAJOR BRANCHES OF METEOROLOGY

SYNOPTIC METEOROLOGY

DYNAMIC METEOROLOGY

WEATHER INSTRUMENTS

Meteorologists use many instruments to gather information about weather. The thermometer, which measures temperature, and the barometer, which measures atmospheric pressure, are some of the oldest and most common weather instruments. Today, satellites in space collect weather information worldwide. Meteorological satellites travel in various orbits and carry a wide variety of sensors. There are two principal types of meteorological satellites—the low-flying polar orbiter and the geostationary orbiter.

POLAR-ORBITING SATELLITES
Polar-orbiting satellites generally orbit at about 520 miles (830 kilometers) above Earth's surface along nearly north-south paths.

GEOSTATIONARY WEATHER SATELLITES
Geostationary weather satellites are at a much greater distance and are directly above the Equator. These orbit just about once a day and in the direction of Earth's rotation, so that they appear to hover over a fixed point on Earth.

HOW FAR ABOVE EARTH'S SURFACE DO GEOSTATIONARY SATELLITES ORBIT?

- **13,400 MILES (21,565 KILOMETERS)**
- **22,300 MILES (35,900 KILOMETERS)**

DISASTER PREPAREDNESS

HISTORY OF FORECASTING

The National Weather Service (NWS), the official weather bureau of the United States, was founded on February 9, 1870, and charged with providing forecasts and warnings to help safeguard the lives and property of American citizens from the dangers of severe weather, as well as to protect the national economy from weather-related disruptions. The NWS maintains an integrated network of more than 100 regional and field offices across the United States and its possessions. Forecasts are derived from weather and climate data collected from a multitude of sources, including satellites, aircraft, weather balloons, and ground-level remote sensing equipment, such as Doppler weather radar. The NWS began with the Signal Service Corps of the U.S. Army. The original purpose of the service was to provide storm warnings for the Atlantic and Gulf coasts and for the Great Lakes.

For more than 100 years, display stations along the coasts of the United States and Puerto Rico and along the shores of the Great Lakes hoisted flags to warn of small craft advisories, gale warnings, storm warnings, and hurricane warnings. Warning flags are still flown in some areas to warn boaters and coastal residents of dangerous weather conditions.

ADVISORIES, WARNINGS, AND WATCHES

Government and military organizations throughout the world issue warnings for all kinds of threatening weather events. In the United States, the National Weather Service provides weather forecasts and warnings.

ADVISORY   **WATCH**   **WARNING**

STORM WARNING

WHEN DID IT HAPPEN?

1970   1960

1951   1816

1870

HOW FAR IN ADVANCE IS A HURRICANE WATCH ISSUED?

36 HOURS   **48 HOURS**   **72 HOURS**

HURRICANES

Forecasting hurricane landfall and providing warnings for storms that will affect the United States is done by the National Hurricane Center in Miami, Florida. Forecasters use a variety of observational information from satellites and aircraft to determine the current location and intensity of the storm. This information is used along with computer forecast models to predict the future path and intensity of the storm.

Before a hurricane arrives, people may need to board up their windows and seek shelter away from the storm.

TORNADOES

Meteorologists can predict when and where tornadoes might form. When weather conditions are likely to result in a tornado, meteorologists announce a tornado watch. When a tornado has been spotted, a tornado warning is issued.

If a tornado is near, people should take shelter in sturdy buildings. Basements and rooms without windows are the safest places. Mobile homes and cars do not offer enough protection. If caught outside, a person should stay close to the ground, preferably in a ditch.

REDUCING EARTHQUAKE HAZARDS

Although earthquakes can cause death and destruction through such secondary effects as landslides, tsunamis, fires, and fault rupture, the greatest losses in terms of both lives and property usually results from the collapse of man-made surface and subsurface structures during the violent shaking of the ground. The most effective way to reduce the destructiveness of earthquakes is to design and construct buildings and other structures capable of withstanding strong shaking.

TSUNAMIS

All low-lying coastal areas are vulnerable to tsunamis. Tsunamis can't be stopped, but there are ways to defend against them. Scientists around the world watch for early signs of earthquakes. They also note unusual changes in ocean levels. With this information, scientists can warn people to leave areas that a tsunami might hit. The generation of a tsunami is rapid, and because of their great speed, the waves can reach shore very quickly.

Anyone who is at the beach or near the ocean and feels the Earth shake should immediately move to higher ground, rather than wait for a warning to be issued. It is not safe to return to low-lying ground until an official "all-clear" has been issued.

THE UNITED STATES HAS TWO REGIONAL TSUNAMI WARNING CENTERS FOR THE PACIFIC OCEAN. WHICH LOCATION DOES *NOT* HAVE ONE OF THE TWO REGIONAL TSUNAMI WARNING CENTERS?

- **HONOLULU, HAWAII**
- **OCEANSIDE, CALIFORNIA**
- **PALMER, ALASKA**

EMERGENCY KITS

An emergency kit could include the following items:

- WATER
- NONPERISHABLE FOOD
- WEATHER RADIO
- FLASHLIGHT AND BATTERIES
- FIRST AID KIT
- WHISTLE
- CAN OPENER
- CELL PHONE WITH CHARGER
- MOIST TOWELETTES

WILD AND WEIRD

NATURAL WONDERS

AURORAS

Auroras are dazzling displays of colored light that sometimes appear in the night sky. They occur in Earth's far northern and far southern regions. In the Northern Hemisphere, such a display is known as aurora borealis, or the northern lights. In the Southern Hemisphere, it is called aurora australis, or the southern lights. Auroras are caused by the sun. The sun sends out a stream of electrically charged particles called the solar wind. The solar wind travels from the sun toward Earth at great speed. Earth is a huge magnet surrounded by a magnetic field. Earth's magnetic field forces the charged particles in the solar wind toward the planet's northern and southern polar regions. The particles move downward through Earth's upper atmosphere. As they do, they crash into atoms and molecules of gases such as oxygen and nitrogen. These collisions cause the atoms and molecules to give off light. This light is an aurora. The different gases that give off the light determine an aurora's colors.

AURORAS ALSO OCCUR ON OTHER PLANETS IN THE SOLAR SYSTEM.

SNOWFLAKES

Snowflakes are collections of ice crystals, which appear in an infinite variety of forms and are often beautifully intricate. The way that ice crystals join together gives every snowflake a unique design. Even so, most snowflakes have six points or six sides. They form seven basic shapes: stars, needles, dendrites (having branches), plates, columns, columns capped with plates, and irregular (damaged). What shape a snowflake takes depends on the temperature and the amount of moisture in the cloud.

Touch an image of a type of snowflake shape on the left. Then touch the matching name on the right.

CAPPED COLUMN

COLUMN

DENDRITE

IRREGULAR

NEEDLE

PLATE

STAR

SNOW ROLLERS

Snow rollers are rare occurrences that only form when certain conditions are met. The ground must be covered by a layer of ice that doesn't allow new snow to adhere. New snow that falls must be wet and sticky, and it also needs to be light and loose enough to be moved by the wind. Finally, the temperature must be near freezing. If all these requirements are met, then winds that are strong, but not too strong, can make a snow roller.

DUST DEVILS

Dust devils, also called sand devils, are small, brief whirlwinds occurring most frequently in the early afternoon when a land surface is heating rapidly. Dust devils are occasionally made visible by the lofting of dust, leaves, or other loose matter from the surface. Observers report dust devils almost daily during the hot season over the Sahara as well as the arid regions of Australia and the southwestern United States. They also are common over sections of India and the Middle East. Dust devils can last from several seconds to several hours and have visible heights ranging from a few feet to more than 4,900 feet (1,500 meters).

BALL LIGHTNING

Ball lightning, also called globe lightning, is a rare aerial phenomenon in the form of a brilliant sphere that is generally several inches in diameter. It usually occurs near the ground during thunderstorms, in close association with cloud-to-ground lightning. It may be red, orange, yellow, white, or blue in color and is often accompanied by a hissing sound and distinct odor. It normally lasts only a few seconds, usually moving about and then vanishing suddenly, either silently or explosively. Ball lightning has been reported to cause damage by burning or melting but is usually harmless. Its causes and its relation to common lightning are not known.

ONE LARGE DUST DEVIL LASTED FOR SEVEN HOURS AS IT TRAVELED 40 MILES (64 KILOMETERS) ON SALT FLATS IN WESTERN UTAH.

EARTH'S EXTREMES

- **GREATEST 24-HOUR RAINFALL:**
  71.8 INCHES (182.37 CENTIMETERS)

- **LONGEST DRY PERIOD:**
  173 MONTHS

- **FASTEST WIND SPEED:**
  253 MILES (407 KILOMETERS) PER HOUR

- **HOTTEST TEMPERATURE:**
  134° F (56.7° C)

- **COLDEST TEMPERATURE:**
  −128.5° F (−89.2° C)

- **HEAVIEST HAILSTONE:**
  2.25 POUNDS (1.02 KILOGRAMS)

REVIEW WHAT YOU KNOW

BY THE NUMBERS

2,200 40 **8**
74 695

What are tropical cyclones that occur in the western North Pacific called?
- HURRICANES
- TYPHOONS

What is the seismically active belt where most volcanoes occur called?
- THE RING OF FIRE
- THE DUST BOWL

Which scale is used to classify tornado intensity?
- ENHANCED FUJITA SCALE
- SAFFIR-SIMPSON SCALE

What is the molten rock flowing on the outside of a volcano called?
- LAVA
- MAGMA

Where was the world's coldest temperature of −128.5° F (−89.2° C) recorded?
- MCMURDO STATION, ANTARCTICA
- VOSTOK STATION, ANTARCTICA

Which type of lightning strikes between the positive and negative charges in different clouds?
- INTRA-CLOUD LIGHTNING
- CLOUD-TO-CLOUD LIGHTNING